Bb is for Bear
A Kodiak Island Alphabet Book
By Cindy Jones

About the Author

Cindy Jones is an early childhood educator and writer living on Kodiak Island, Alaska. She collects alphabet books and has made one each year with her tiny students. Cindy loves to explore and discover through play with her students. She is an avid reader, hiker, and traveler. She is a curious, lifelong learner and spends her time with her husband, three adult children, her friends, and her dog and cat.

Photos for the title page, Bb is for bear and Nn is for northern lights taken by Kris Luckenbach. Check out his amazing work at krisluckphoto.com.

Follow Cindy at the Kodiak Compass Classroom and @cindiannajones

This book is dedicated to my mom who gave me an example of a reader, brought me to the library, and bought me book club subscriptions that inspired my love of alphabet books and reading.

Bb is for bear

Ee is for eagle

Ii is for irises

Jj is for jellyfish

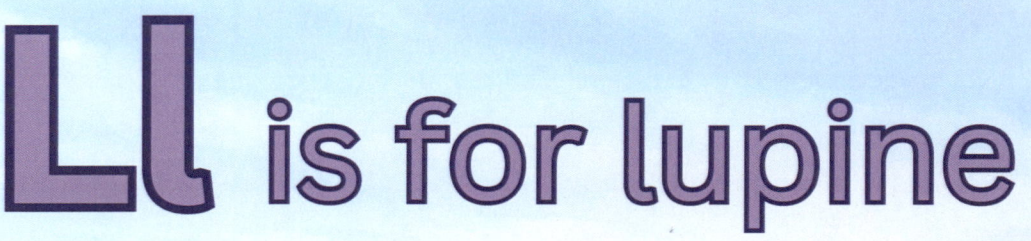

Ll is for lupine

Mm is for moss

Oo is for octopus

Pp is for puffin

Qq
is for Qik'rtaq
(Alutiiq for Kodiak Island)

Tt
is for the Three Sisters

Ww is for whale

Yy is for yarrow

www.ingramcontent.com/pod-product-compliance
Lightning Source LLC
Chambersburg PA
CBRC101144030426
42337CB00009B/70